LESSONS FROM THE
FIERY FURNACE

*Pearls of Wisdom From My Own Life's
Challenges to Help You Overcome ANY
Obstacle in Your Path*

CHRISTINA M. STIMSON, M.D.

LESSONS FROM THE FIERY FURNACE

Unless otherwise noted, all Scripture quotations are from the
New American Standard Bible (1995 update).
Scripture quotations marked NKJV are from the New King James
Version. http://www.Biblegateway.com (accessed June 2008)
Scripture quotations marked NLT are from the New Living Translation.
http://www.Biblegateway.com (accessed June 2008)

Where proper names are in quotation marks they have been changed
and do not represent the actual first name.

Published for Worldwide Distribution by:

QUEST PUBLICATIONS
6-176 Henry Street
Brantford, Ontario, N3S 5C8
Canada
Email: questpublications@outlook.com
Website: www.questpub.questforgod.org

Cover Design & Interior Layout / Formatting by:

QUEST PUBLICATIONS

ISBN 978-1-988439-09-9

Printed In The United States Of America

"And they overcame him because of the blood of the Lamb and because of the word of their testimony."

—Revelation 12:11

DEDICATION

This book is dedicated to my Beloved Precious Golden Retriever, Honey Bear, who saw me through tremendous difficulties in my life and who is the biggest blessing in my life!

I also want to thank very much Lee Grizzard for her tireless efforts in editing my manuscript, for her encouragement, support, and friendship as well.

And to all the hurting hearts out there who may be reading this book: My prayer is for the Lord to bring total healing and restoration to every hurt. God loves you! You are valuable and special to Him.

I hope this book helps you on your journey. You are loved with an everlasting love!

TABLE OF CONTENTS

CHAPTER ONE

MY TESTIMONY...MY OWN FIERY FURNACE

This book is about providing you with hope and the tools to overcoming in life. No matter what your problem or how dire your situation; our God can pierce the darkness with His magnificent light. I should know. I lived a nightmare for the first six decades of my life. And just as the Lord brought me through all of what you are about to read, I pray you will come to agree He can bring you through anything.

Matthew 10:26: "For I came to set a man against his father, and a daughter against her mother, and a daughter-in-law against her mother-in-law; and a man's enemies will be the members of His household."

The circumstances in which I grew up were extremely challenging. I was physically hit, abused and yelled at very often. My mother had an extremely difficult time coping raising children and I believe had a severe, undiagnosed and untreated mental health issue which was suggested by my own mental health professional as being paranoid schizophrenia. She exhibited intense anger and rage issues on a daily basis.

I did not know when the door of my bedroom would get banged down and this would occur. I lived in constant fear and anxiety. I do recall as a little child scotch taping wads of Kleenex on my body in the futile hopes of not feeling as much pain when being hit.

In my view she treated my three brothers with far more respect than me, something that appeared to be "handed-down" from her own Greek mother. Apparently in Ancient Greece, only males were considered valued, not females.

As a consequence of this I had no self-esteem and inner confidence growing up, no sense of being safe or secure, just constant chaos. In addition, I learned at a young age to perform faultlessly well in school and get straight A's in a futile attempt to appease my mom's aggression, trying to win her love and improve my own self-worth, or so I thought. In short, I did whatever I could to stay under the radar screen growing up so I would not "be a problem" for my Mom. Deep inside, of course, as a little girl, I desperately longed for a close, loving, supportive, non-threatening relationship with my Mom that I saw my other friends have. By the grace of God, many years later this did happen which is described later in another chapter.

Growing up my father, however, was my ego support. I lived to try to please him. He insisted I go to college and "make something of myself."

I had wanted to be a teacher, but at the time, there were a glut of teachers. When I then chose acting as my major my father refused to support me to study acting. He thought I would starve as an actress. My father grew up during the Depression and in his experience doctors were the ones who had food on their tables for they bartered their services for food. He therefore insisted I become a doctor, very much against my own will. It was no small task, after all!

I was accepted to medical school and around that time met a man who was also of Mediterranean descent. He was an attorney and he represented prominent ball players. My father detested him and said I should have nothing to do with him. However, because I had no self-esteem, I was thankful that someone "loved" me and paid attention to me. I had feared remaining single my whole life. My father had told me I would rue the day I married this man, but because I was deeply insecure and because I resented my father's control over my life, I married him anyway. Later, I understood my father's concerns.

Indeed, marrying him took me from the proverbial frying pan into the fire. The only silver lining to this very dark cloud was that his mother led me to the Lord in an Assembly of God prayer meeting. I received the Baptism of the Holy Spirit there and felt such great peace for the first time in my life. This newfound relationship with the Holy Spirit helped me survive what was to come.

My new husband, "Peter", insisted I finish medical school, become a doctor and complete a residency. I did not want to do this. It was never my dream to become a doctor...only my father's.

Now my husband had that same goal for me and would not hear of me quitting to "just be a wife." In retrospect he seemed to enjoy taking me around to his professional athlete clients and showing me off like a trophy because I was a doctor. This was quite embarrassing for me.

After several years of marriage, I learned that my husband was into very dark things. Without my knowledge he had accrued nearly one million dollars in Internal Revenue Service debt as well as $350,000 in credit card debt with 37 credit cards that had been "jointly assigned" which encumbered me, also. When his professional ball players left him due to his financial mismanagement he wanted to take his severance funds and hide them from the IRS. Everything within me said "No, you must not do this!" and I objected strongly.

Not long thereafter I was forcefully abducted from my home by my husband colluding with my own brother (who became a business associate of my husband) and one of his brothers, held against my will, subject to abuse and persecuted for wanting to tell the truth and pay the taxes owed. My employer and friends did not know where I was. "Peter" told them I had taken a much needed vacation. He also picked up my last paycheck from my employer. After two months of captivity I was able to escape my abductors. I returned home and grabbed the $300 I had stuffed under a mattress and bought a one-way ticket out of there.

My choices of where to go were very limited. I decided to go stay with my parents who had moved to a different state. This was not easy for them or me. My father was livid because his preconceptions about my husband had been accurate.

I knew nothing else so I had to keep dancing…get my medical license, earn some money, get out of the house and begin a new life for myself.

In the course of attempting to do this I was diagnosed with cervical cancer, which was a consequence of my husband's infidelity and the human papilloma virus (HPV) cervical infection I had contracted from him. I subsequently found out he was involved with prostitutes. Moreover, while trying to obtain a divorce and deal with all the IRS proceedings and credit card debt I developed lupus. I became so sick at work one day I had to be carried home on a stretcher from the clinic. I had developed profound chest pains… lupus pleuritis… and very severe weakness in my upper extremities. As if this were not enough I also had to have emergency abdominal surgery for horrific pain from extensive pelvic endometriosis. It was at this point in my life I finally said to the Lord: "Please take over my life. Everyone else has tried to run my life except you. Your Word says in Jeremiah that you have plans to prosper me and not to harm me, to give me a future and a hope." (Jeremiah 29:11) I had nothing to my name but God. I felt like not only did I have the trials of Job but also had a life like Joseph of Genesis being thrown into a pit. Slowly but surely, the Lord turned my life around. My ex-husband's own family members gave me sworn affidavits describing his grievous financial dealings. Armed with those affidavits and with my father's much-needed assistance, I was granted an Innocent Spouse verdict by the IRS so that I was not obligated to pay one penny of the taxes my former husband owed. Through my own diligent efforts to microfiche all 37 credit cards and prove that the signature of my name was not my own, but a forged one, I was discharged from the credit card debts as well.

I received treatment for the cervical cancer. The lupus symptoms came under relatively good control with medication and prayer. Slowly but surely I was able to come up for air.

In time, the Lord restored not only my physical health, but my emotional health as well. Not surprisingly I undertook major psychological counseling. God provided me with a wonderful Christian psychologist to help me cope and heal inside. And above all the Lord provided me with precious Golden Retrievers ALL along the way that helped my heart heal so much as I came to understand the unconditional love, support, comfort, acceptance and peace that ONLY an animal companions can bring. I was never even allowed to have dogs in my life growing up, but when I met my second husband, thank God all that changed. He introduced me to the absolute best friends in my life....My Precious Golden Retrievers!

In my opinion, there was and is nothing that brings such joy to my heart than to be around the true loves of my life...my Beloved Golden Retrievers. My life was blessed to have Jockey, my first Golden Retriever who was a retired Guide Dog of the Blind. Then I had Chip whom I rescued from Roseburg, Oregon and my One and Only Precious Most Beloved Golden of ALL time in my life... Honey Bear whom I adopted from Estacada, Oregon.

Honey Bear ended up saving my life. As mentioned, I had gotten remarried many years after the above mentioned ordeal and did not realize that I would have many more problems in my second marriage. Honey Bear is my lifeline and ended up saving my life. I had gotten so very drastically physically ill from a lot of unnecessary stress I had gone through with my second husband, that I nearly died. By the Grace of God, I recovered my health.

During that time, however, of being so physically ill, I could not pray, I could not read the Bible, I could not do anything but hope to God I would someday get my physical health improved. The Lord had touched and healed Honey Bear after I noticed something was wrong in her abdomen, that her spleen needed removing. When I saw the Lord healed Honey Bear I had the faith to believe He could heal me. And he did.

Slowly but surely, the Lord turned my life around. Furthermore, and very importantly, I praise the Lord for bringing the much needed restoration and healing to both my mother's and my relationship as well as that of my present husband. It is all the result of His hand which guided and restored these relationships And it all happened by walking in forgiveness.

The Lord is no respecter of persons. If He did this for me, He can and will most certainly restore what you need in your life. He will give you a "crown of beauty for ashes" (Isaiah 61:3, NKJV). He will "make up to you for the years that the swarming locust has eaten." (Joel 2:25).

So it is on this basis I write this book…to help empower you, no matter where you are on your journey. The Lord is more than able to carry you and He will if you let Him. He will bring you through your own fiery furnace, and I pray He will be able to use insights in this book to help you along your way.

CHAPTER TWO

LIVE YOUR OWN LIFE

No one is more qualified than you to live your dreams!

If there were only one thing I only wish I could do over in my own life, it would be to make my **own** decisions and not allow anyone else to make them for me. Growing up in an extremely dysfunctional home and suffering severe emotional and physical abuse, I gave to other people my right to make my own decisions. I did not have an intact sense of self-esteem and there were people in my life who, because of their controlling natures, were only too willing to make my decisions for me. Over this, I have MUCH regret!

In my own life, my father and another aunt, albeit very well meaning, insisted I become a doctor. How easy for them to be adamant about this goal. Neither one of them would have to do the work. Yet neither one of them would relent. I experienced much family pressure to measure up and tow this mark. All the while, my heart was telling me NOT to do it. I felt like a lamb going to slaughter. In retrospect, it is amazing what I did to gain the approval of others.

I only wish at that time I had had enough back-bone in me to say "NO!" You DO have choices and the right to make your own decisions and live with the results. You must live your **own** dream and not allow anyone or anything to steal this from you.

If you have accepted Jesus Christ as your Lord and Savior, the Holy Spirit is your guide and will always lead you into truth. (John 16:13) You must trust the Holy Spirit as He guides you. Scripture tells us in Isaiah 30:21 "Your ears will hear a word behind you, 'This is the way, walk in it,' whenever you turn to the right or to the left." Psalm 32:8 states "I will instruct you and teach you in the way which you should go. I will counsel you with My eye upon you."

The Holy Spirit speaks to our hearts and we need to trust Him in that leading. James 1:5-8 admonishes "But if any of you lacks wisdom, let him ask of God, who gives to all men generously and without reproach, and it will be given to him. But he must ask in faith without any doubting, for the one who doubts is like the surf of the sea driven and tossed by the wind. For that man ought not to expect that he will receive anything from the Lord, being a double-minded man, unstable in all his ways."

So what happens as a result of not living your own dream? At the very least, you will experience a lot of frustration, disappointment and heartache. The Lord God made you with unique gifts and talents that He wants you to discover, develop, and use for His glory. These are God-given and no one has the right to take this from you and steal what the Lord plants in your own heart. You must follow your own path and chart your own course under the guidance of the Holy Spirit. Then you will be fruitful and have peace.

As you read this if you find that you are at a crossroad, particularly if it is a life-changing decision such as what career you will pursue or whom you will marry, wait upon the Lord and He will guide you by the power of the Holy Spirit speaking to your heart. Do not make any decision until you are led by His peace regarding the matter. Move forward on what He tells you to do only after you have His peace. And allow no one to tell you otherwise.

CHAPTER THREE

THE ANCHOR OF YOUR SOUL...
CHRIST AND HIS WORD

It has been said that we know the value of an anchor only when we are in the storm. The purpose of this book is to provide the tools for you to know how to be an overcomer in your own life. For myself and countless others, faith in Jesus Christ and His Word, the Bible, is our anchor. I only wish I had learned earlier in my own life the value of knowing Christ as my Savior and Lord and His Word.

Why is this important? Because knowing who you are in Christ and understanding the authority you have been given through His shed blood are tantamount to overcoming in life. When Christ died on the Cross at Calvary His death purchased; peace, joy, restoration, healing and provision for all of our needs. The Gospel of John 10:10 tells us "The thief comes only to steal, kill and destroy, but I (Jesus) came that they may have life and have it more abundantly." Hosea 4:6 tell us "God's people are destroyed for lack of knowledge." It is so important to study, meditate on and familiarize yourself with the powerful Word of God. Jeremiah 29:11 states "For I know the plans I have for you, declares the Lord, plans for welfare and not calamity, plans to give you a hope and a future."

True inner healing comes when you replace any lies or negative tapes told to you from childhood with the truth of God's Word and what He says about you.

Because my mother had a severe mental illness she inflicted horrific physical and emotional abuse day in and day out as I was growing up. In the course of being on the receiving end of this abuse, I had come to believe very negative things about myself. When I accepted the Lord in my life, I learned to replace all the lies of the enemy that were perpetrated on me as a young girl with His truths. And slowly but surely I regained my sense of self-esteem that had been stolen from me. Your self-talk is very important, especially if you are trying to recover from the highly damaging effects of being the victim of abuse.

As a child of God you are loved by God and you are very special to Him. You have a rich spiritual inheritance. You are seated spiritually with Christ in the heavenly places and are considered a joint heir with Him. You are a blood-bought child of the Living God, purchased with a price, adopted as His child, made in His image and for fellowship and intimacy with Him and, thus, you have infinite worth and value. In addition you have been given all power and authority over all the works of darkness. So have confidence in God because He has a good plan for your life. You will find your soul comforted as you spend time in the Word of God and meditate on the Scriptures. That is how your mind is renewed and transformed, by reading and meditating on the Word of God.

It is very true that the battlefield is the mind so we need to be careful to take every thought captive unto Christ. We need to be sure that our thoughts and our confessions line up with the Word of God.

Proverbs 23:7 states, "For as he (a man) thinks within himself, so he is." And Proverbs 18:21 says "Death and life are in the power of the tongue and those who love it will eats its fruit." Christ called you and me to freedom. We need to be on guard against the tactics of the enemy affecting our thought-life. For example, the enemy's tactics include fear, insecurity, rejection and discouragement. As you arm yourself with the Word of God you will overcome all the tactics of the enemy and live a life of victory.

We are all in an unseen battle. "For out struggle not against flesh and blood, but against the rulers, against the powers, against the world forces of this darkness, against the spiritual forces of wickedness in the heavenly places." (Ephesians 6:12) In order to overcome the enemy and his tactics, we need to know who we are in Christ.

WHO YOU ARE IN CHRIST

YOU ARE....
A child of God (Romans 8:16)
Redeemed from the hand of the enemy (Psalm 107:2)
Forgiven (Colossians 1:13-14)
Saved by Grace through Faith (Ephesians 2:8)
Justified (Romans 5:11)
Sanctified (I Corinthians. 6:11)
A new creature (II Corinthians. 5:17)
Partaker of His divine nature (2 Peter 1:4)
Created in His image (Genesis 1:27)
Redeemed from the curse of the law (Galatians 3:13)
Led by the Spirit of God (Romans 8:14)
A Son (Daughter) of God (Romans 8:14)
Kept in safety wherever you go (Psalm 91:11)
Having all your needs met by Jesus (Philippians 4:19)

Casting ALL your cares on Jesus (I Peter 5:7)

Strong in the Lord and the Power of His might (Ephesians 6:10)

Doing ALL things through Christ who strengthens you (Philippians 4:13)

An heir with God and a joint-heir with Christ (Romans 8:17)

Heir to the blessings of Abraham (Galatians 3:13-14)

Observing and doing the Lord's commandments (Deuteronomy 28:12)

Blessed coming in and going out (Deuteronomy28:6)

An inheritor of eternal life (I John 5: 11-12) Blessed with all spiritual blessings (Ephesians 1:3)

Healed by His stripes (I Peter 2:24) Exercising your authority over the enemy (Luke 10:19)

Above only and NOT underneath (Deuteronomy 28:13)

More than a conqueror (Romans 8:37)

Establishing God's Word here on earth (Matthew 16:19)

An overcomer by the Blood of the Lamb and the Word of your Testimony (Romans 12:11)

Daily overcoming the devil (I John 4:4)

Not moved by what you see (II Corinthians. 4:18)

Walking by faith and not by sight (II Corinthians 5:7)

Casting down imaginations and bringing every thought captive unto the obedience of Christ. (II Corinthians 10:4-5)

Being transformed by a renewed mind (Romans 12:1-2)

A co-laborer with God (I Corinthians. 3:9) The righteousness of God in Christ Jesus (II Corinthians. 5:21)

An imitator of Jesus (Ephesians 5:12)

A chosen race, a royal priesthood, a holy nation, a people for God's own possession (I Peter 2:9)

The light of the world (Matthew 5:14)

Storms are apart of life here on earth. When you are going through a storm it can shake you to the core of your being. What will you hold on to? To what will you anchor your soul? Find Scriptures that pertain to your situation and what you are going through and anchor them to your soul.

God's Word states that His Word does not return empty without accomplishing what He desires. (Isaiah 55:11) When going through storms try to keep in mind Romans 8:28: "And we know that God causes all things to work together for good to those who love God, to those who are called according to His purpose." Clearly not everything that happens to us is good, because of our own sin or the sins of others. But even the bad things work for our good if we submit ourselves, our lives to God. He will make our trials become our testimonies as we walk through our storms with Him at our side. You are never alone! You always have the Holy Spirit to guide you and comfort you if you have accepted Christ as your Lord and Savior. If you need comfort the Psalms are especially good at soothing the soul.

There are small booklets available at every Christian bookstore and online on Bible Promises for every need: financial provision, emotional and physical restoration, dealing with fear, needing guidance, wisdom, protection, encouragement, and deliverance, etc. We have a big God and His arms are big enough to carry you through whatever you are experiencing. He wants you to lean on Him and His Word, as you trust Him to work out your circumstances.

God's Word is powerful! Hebrews 4:12 states "The word of God is living and active and sharper than any two-edged sword and piercing as far as the division of soul and spirit, of both joints and marrow, and able to judge the thoughts and the intentions of the heart."

There are so many examples I could share with you on the power of standing on God's Word and using that as your spiritual weapon. God's Word is actually part of your armor. In Ephesians 5 we are taught to put on the whole armor of God. The Word of God is the only offensive weapon in that armor. Remember in Genesis, God spoke creation into existence and brought order out of chaos. Similarly He wants us to speak to our circumstances.

Are there mountains you would like to see moved from your life? Start speaking to them! Jesus Himself taught this as recounted in the Gospel of Mark. And Jesus answered saying to them "Have faith in God. Truly I say to you, whoever says to this mountain, be taken up and cast into the sea' and does not doubt in his heart, but believes that what he says is going to happen, it shall be granted him. Therefore, I say to you all things for which you pray and ask, believe that you have received them, and they will be granted you." (Mark 11:22-24).

Are you suffering from a physical infirmity? The Lord brought me through years of suffering with incredibly painful lupus pleuritis, or chest pains, as I just kept speaking the Word of God and believing it to be true. The Word of God tells us in Isaiah 53 that when Jesus went to the Cross He took our infirmities and diseases upon His body.

"Surely our grief's He Himself bore, and our sorrows He carried; yet we ourselves esteemed Him stricken, smitten of God and afflicted. But He was pierced through for our transgressions; He was crushed for our iniquities. The chastening for our well-being fell upon Him, and by His scourging we are healed." (Isaiah 53: 4, 5).

Psalm 107:20 states "He sent His word and healed them." You need to know that you have a God, the Lord Jesus Christ who wants to heal your body as well as your soul. And once again, if He did this for me, He can and will do this for you.

Start speaking the Word of God and you will see circumstances in your life change for the better. Live from God's promises, not from your circumstances.

Remember Proverbs 18:21 tells us "Death and life are in the power of the tongue and those who love it will eat its fruit."

I want to tell you a true story of a woman I was asked to pray for with a very serious and life-threatening disease called myelofibrosis. In this condition her bone marrow was not producing normal blood cells, but highly abnormal ones. I was asked by a friend to accompany her to pray for this mother of five. When I saw the woman she was in her early 40's and I knew without a miracle, an intervention of the Lord, that she was at death's door. Since God's Word says it pierces to the bone marrow I knew that I could claim her total physical healing based upon the finished work of the Cross and what the Lord did for her two thousand years ago. He is the same yesterday, today and forever. I prayed for the healing of the myelofibrosis and I prayed the finished to work of the Cross and Jesus' healing upon this woman's life.

One month later she phoned me to tell me her physician at the renowned M.D. Anderson Medical Center told her she had no sign of myelofibrosis in her bone marrow and that he did not need to see her anymore. When I later saw the woman in person her health had so greatly improved that I have to tell you I did not recognize her! God truly touched her and brought a full measure of healing to her body. That was in August of 2007 and she has been well ever since. Again, if He did this for her He can do this for you, too.

I recall a miracle of the Lord's healing touch I witnessed firsthand in medical school. There was a little boy, around three or four years old who was paralyzed. I was rotating through the neurology clerkship at the time. Having recently accepted the Lord Jesus into my own heart just prior to medical school I quietly went to this little boy's room and said a prayer over him, asking the Lord to touch and heal him. Imagine my amazement when the boy arose in his little crib and stood up! He had never been able to do that before. He even took some steps! So before my very eyes the Lord demonstrated His miracle-working power in that little boy.

One example in my own life of both emotional and physical healing was when I stood on God's Word in Joel 2:25 that He would make up for the years in my life the locusts ate. He did. Although I came from a horrible home life and went to an even worse marriage, in time the Lord restored my life, allowed me the opportunity to minister His Word to the sick and wounded. The Lord completely turned my life around, and redeemed my life from the pit! It did not happen overnight, but it did happen by standing, praying and believing the Word of God to be true. God's Word is truth… eternal truth! God cannot lie. His Word is the perfect anchor for whatever storm comes against your life. And He wants to heal, restore and redeem any and all pain you have experienced in your own life and turn it around for good, be it physical, emotional or spiritual. He wants to heal you at the very core of your being.

Even medical science recognizes that sometimes our physical problems are related to what we are experiencing emotionally. As I mentioned previously, I experienced severe lupus symptoms, which were a veritable rejection of my own body tissues by my immune system. What was transpiring in my life in an emotionally paralleling circumstance was the extreme physical rejection I had experienced at the hands of my mother. So sometimes there are physical correlates of spiritual and emotional disease.

The Lord brought healing to both. He delights in doing this. His Word states in III John 1:2 "Beloved I pray that in all respects you may prosper and be in good health, just as your soul prospers."

Christ wants to heal and restore us in every realm......mentally, physically, emotionally and spiritually. He wants you to be whole and happy and live a fulfilled life. The only way I believe we can do this is to make Him the anchor of our soul and our life. He can turn the most dire situation around. As I have said before, He did this for me and if He did this for me He can and will do this for you, too!

"Bless the Lord, O my soul; And all that is within me, bless His holy name.

Bless the Lord, O my soul, And forget none of His benefits;

Who pardons all your iniquities;

Who heals all your diseases;

Who redeems your life from the pit;

Who crowns you with loving kindness and compassion;

Who satisfies your years with good things,

So that your youth is renewed like the eagle."

—Psalm 103

CHAPTER FOUR

CULTIVATE THE GARDEN OF YOUR HEART TO BRING HEALING FOR YOUR SOUL

Your heart is like a garden. What do you want planted there? You can choose between flowers and weeds…healthy relationships and toxic ones.

Who do you want sowing into your life? Are the people in your circle of friends cultivating the soil of your heart and planting good seeds? Or do some of your relationships need a bit of weeding and pruning? Friendships are so important! We all need people we can trust and with whom we can be safe. And this is a two-way street. It is really true that to have friends we need to become friends to people.

I like to watch carefully who is in my life and to whom I entrust my heart and my prayers. You want to surround yourself with people who will build you up, encourage and support you…not tear you down. The Lord tells us in His Word to bear one another's burdens so He expects us to be able to have good friends in our lives to whom we can turn. Friends who can offer a good listening ear, guidance and prayer support no matter what we are going through are priceless. But we need to limit the amount of contact controlling or otherwise unhealthy people have in our lives if we want to be emotionally and physically healthy ourselves.

The Bible states that 'death and life are in the power of the tongue and those who love it will eat it's fruit." Our words are very important and must be chosen carefully....both what we speak into other people and what we receive. We want to bless others with our words, not send curses. The same is true of people we allow in our own lives. We need people around us who will speak life, not death, into our lives.

Friends can be very comforting to us, particularly as we encounter the storms of life. Storms can rage at times. In addition to the anchor of God's Word are godly, Christian friends who can love and support you in your time of need. I am very grateful I had them through my rough times. They were very good sounding boards and helped me cope with the many problems I was facing.

So examine your life today and eliminate any toxic weeds from the garden of your heart. Pray for the Lord to bring into your life good, loving, caring friends who will support you and give you godly counsel.

In addition, consider finding a mentor… someone to whom you look up to and someone who shares your Christian values and can help you along your life's journey. Mentors are so valuable and helpful! I had several and I thank the Lord for each one. In my own particular situation I needed caring, compassionate, positive female role models because of the toxic maternal parenting I had. I needed to learn that it was okay to trust women and that not all women were like my own. mother. I thank God for those women! So mentors can be quite helpful and supportive to you and I highly recommend them.

CHAPTER FIVE

YOUR CHURCH...HELP FOR THE HURTING

Churches, made up of people, are not perfect. They are a place to receive good Bible-based teaching as well as connecting with other people of similar faith. In addition, some churches offer Bible-based counseling and programs to help with various problems such as addictions and relationship issues. If you have come from a dysfunctional home, a healthy church or online Christian group can be a vital link to experiencing validation, hope, and the love of Christ. You are God's child and He loves you.

In choosing the right church or Christian fellowship group...either the actual physical place or online here are some consideration:

~How welcome do you feel when you are there? ~Are you comfortable with their style of worship?

~What Sunday school classes/educational opportunities are available to learn and grow in your faith?

~And very importantly, do their beliefs align with God's Word?

~Do their messages speak to your heart, uplift and encourage you in your faith?

~Don't be afraid to try different churches or other Christian groups online, etc., until you find the one that is right for you.

One very important consideration (which takes time to develop) is the friendships you will acquire there. The Pastor or minister's sermons can be good but to want to stay at the church it is important to cultivate healthy, godly relationships and friendships with people there as well. Remember that churches are like hospitals for the hurting so don't expect perfection there, in either the pastoral staff or the people in the congregation. Prayerfully, however, it should be a place to learn and grow as a believer, a place to fellowship with other Christians, and a place to give thanks and praise to the Lord.

CHAPTER SIX

GODLY CHRISTIAN COUNSELING...HELP FOR THE HURTING

I cannot stress enough the importance of seeking counseling when you are hurting emotionally. We all have baggage. Some of us like myself have more than others. For me counseling was invaluable! How else could I sort out the deep issues affecting my life and make sense of what I had experienced?

When you have the right counselor and undertake counseling you are opening yourself up so your hurts can be healed. This is what you should receive from a good professional Christian counselor. It takes time, prayer, and a lot of understanding.

The Lord wants you whole and healthy in every dimension. His Word states in Psalm 147:3 "He heals the brokenhearted and binds up their wounds." For the vast majority of people this does not happen by some instantaneous miracle but by working things out emotionally and trying to grow past our pain and learn from our traumas and life experiences. An objective professional counselor can help you do this. One that is Biblically based can help you sort out your life based on the principles in the Word of God, by applying principles like forgiveness.

For the Christian nothing happens by accident or without God's notice. As awful as my childhood was, and first/prior marriage was, God had and has His redemptive purposes in it. The Bible states in Romans 8:28 "And we know that God causes all things work together for good to those who love the Lord, who are called according to

His purpose." Not all things that happen to us are good...that is for sure. And not all things that happen to us are caused by God. He has given all people free will and as a result sin abounds. But He can work even the harm for our good as we submit our lives to Jesus.

As I look back on my own life, one of the most valuable experiences I had was going through counseling. I could count on running in there weekly with whatever trauma I was experiening and the talk therapy really helped me sort things out.

Counseling is so beneficial and there is nothing to be ashamed about in undertaking it. This is how you grow. Emotional healing often occurs like an upward spiral staircase, not usually linearly. Value yourself enough to submit to this process and your soul can receive the healing it needs.

The key is finding the right counselor for you. Ask the Holy Spirit for wisdom in choosing a counselor. Ask your friends or your church for some recommendations and then go check them out for yourself and see what seems right for you. The Lord will guide you as you seek His wisdom and guidance in finding the right professional for you. If money or lack of insurance is an issue, very often churches and some counselors offer counseling on a sliding-scale basis where you pay what you can, if you can. The point is God wants any and all hurts to be healed and seeking professional Christian counseling is an excellent starting point. Only God and you know the trauma you have personally experienced and the healing you seek takes time, so please be patient as you pursue wholeness in Christ.

CHAPTER SEVEN

NEVER GIVE UP! THE IMPORTANCE OF PERSEVERANCE

There are countless examples in the Bible of people who stood in faith and looked to the Lord to turn their circumstances around for the better. Job is just one example, but a very good role model for us. Everything was taken from Job: his family, his possessions, his livelihood, his good health, and yet he continued to trust in God and did not give up. And God turned things around for him and his family.

By now you are familiar with my own story. As I stood through my fiery furnace the Lord turned everything around for the better. It did NOT hap-pen overnight. But I kept the faith and the Lord saw me through each and every time. He is a faithful God and He seeks to do the same in **your** life.

Psalm 119:92, 93 states: "If Your law had not been my delight, then I would have perished in my affliction. I will never forget Your precepts, for by them You have revived me."

Job himself in the middle of his trials states: "Though He slay me, yet I will trust Him." (Job 13:15, NKJV)

How many people out there have given up too quickly and thrown in the towel instead of allowing the Lord to intervene and bring a divine reversal of circumstances? How many people have committed suicide for this reason and just given up? How many frustrated people have committed a crime out of desperation and are now occupying a prison? The list goes on and on.

Look at the life of Joseph in the book of Genesis. His brothers sold him into slavery at a very young age. While in slavery, he was thrown into prison for a false accusation. But over a period of many years, the Lord restored everything he had lost and he became second in line of command in Egypt. What if Joseph had given up prematurely?

He could have said to himself "Well, I sure don't see God in any of this, I might as well give up."

He may have thought that, but he did not act on it. He trusted God instead to turn his circumstances around for good, which eventually is what happened. Significantly, as he persevered he also forgave his brothers and was able to save his family from starvation.

The ability to persevere and keep our faith strong goes hand in hand. Are you experiencing some difficult times right now as you read this?

Don't give up!

What does God's Word tells us about keeping faith in those hard times? Hebrews 11:1 (NKJV) tells us, "Now faith is the substance of things hoped for, the evidence of things not seen." He- brews 11:6 (NKJV) tells us "But without faith it is impossible to please Him, for he who comes to God must believe that He is, and that He is a rewarder of those who diligently seek Him."

Our Lord is right there with you, even if you are walking through some rough times right now.

In Isaiah 43:2 God says, "When you pass through the waters, I will be with you; and through the rivers, they shall not overflow you. When you walk through the fire, you will not be scorched, nor will the flame burn you."

We all have a choice. We can either choose to focus on the Lord and His Word in faith, and trust and persevere in the hard places, or we can look at the waves and the circumstances and become fear-ful. Which do you suppose the Lord wants you to do right now? As the beloved Pastor Joel Osteen says: "Choose to dig in your heels" and make a statement to the devil that you are not going to give up no matter what. Make the right choice to walk by faith and not by sight and He will make your path straight. Proverbs 3:5,6

Hold onto the Word of God with everything in you and never, never give up! Hold on through your tears and heartache no matter how difficult things become. Seek the Lord through His Word and remember to find those Scriptures that pertain to your particular situation. Anchor them to your soul so you will be prepared and will endure during the storms of life. Learn to meditate on His Word as naturally as you live and breathe. The Lord is your shelter, rock, fortress, healer, deliverer, shepherd and encourager of your soul. After you have done all you can possibly do, and after you have prayed tenaciously about the situation, enter into the rest of the Lord and allow Him to fight your battles. He will never leave you or forsake you. Keep the faith, above all, and stand firm in that faith. He will see you through.

"Let us hold fast the confession of our hope without wavering, for He who promised is faithful." (Hebrews 10:23)

CHAPTER EIGHT

FROM ASHES TO BEAUTY...
THE POWER OF WALKING IN FORGIVENESS, AND HE WILL RESTORE THE WASTED YEARS!

In the life of Joseph what the enemy intended against him for evil, God turned around for good for the purpose of saving many souls. Genesis 50:20 (NLT) state "You intended to harm me, but God intended it all for good. He brought me to this position so I could save the lives of many people."

He did the same for me and He can do the same for you.

We all go through tests and trials. They are not fun, but our tests do become our testimonies. And Revelation 12:11 tells us "we overcome by the Blood of the Lamb and by the word of our testimony." Nothing happens to a Christian that does not first go through the filter of the Lord. Romans 8:28 good to those who love God, to those who are called according to His purpose." Clearly not all things that happen to us are good, but He will work them for our good as we submit our lives to Christ.

Our God will restore the wasted years! In the midst of your pain the Lord can give you a vision of the testimony you will have for Him after He delivers you from the trial. He will use everything the enemy intended against you for evil and turn it around for your good.

God's Word tells us, "… you belong to God, my dear children. You have already won a victory over those people because the Spirit who lives in you, "greater is He who lives within you than he that is in this world ." (I John 4:4 NLT)

Jesus already defeated the devil and His Spirit lives on inside of you if you have chosen to accept Him as Lord and Savior. No situation is impossible to turn around, as you believe Him to do so.

Psalm 90:15 states; "Make us glad according to the days You have afflicted us, and the years we have seen evil." In Joel 2:25 God's Word states that He will "make up to for the years that the swarming locust has eaten…"

I am glad and relieved that at many low points in my life the Lord did not show me a panoramic view of what else would happen to me. I would have fainted for sure! But instead He gave me beauty for ashes and He can and will do the same for you as you hold onto Him and the hope of His Word. The Lord restored my physical and emotional health, and of course, my precious Golden Retriever, Honey Bear.

One of my favorite Scripture verses is Isaiah: 61:1-3: "The Spirit of the Lord God is upon me, because the Lord has anointed me to bring good news to the afflicted. He has sent me to bind up the broken hearted, to proclaim liberty to captives, And freedom to prisoners, To proclaim the favorable year of the Lord, And the day of vengeance of our God; To comfort all who mourn, To grant those who mourn in Zion, Giving them a garland (beauty) instead of ashes, The oil of gladness instead of mourning, the mantle of praise instead of a spirit of fainting, So they will be called oaks of righteousness, The planting of the Lord, that He may be glorified."

In my own life, one of the yearnings of my heart was to have my broken heart healed. I felt I had been through about as much rejection as anyone could take. But I knew what Isaiah 61:3 says.

And I knew that Psalm 147:3 states "He heals the brokenhearted and binds up their wounds." I found that healing occurs first with the head knowledge and then gradually moves to the heart. There is healing in forgiving and choosing to let go. In fact, God commands us to do this. If we don't forgive others He won't forgive us. In His kingdom, exercising forgiveness is not an option, but a command. Leave Him to deal with your enemies and He will, for His Word tells us He will. "Never take your own revenge, beloved, but leave room for the wrath of God, for it is written, **"Vengeance is mine,** I WILL REPAY," says the Lord." (Romans 12:19, emphasis added).

Forgiveness is not the same as trust. We choose to forgive our enemies but that does not mean necessarily that we trust them again. In fact, we are called to be as wise as serpents, but as gentle as doves. "Behold I send you out as sheep in the midst of wolves; so be shrewd as serpents and innocent as doves. " (Matthew 10:16).

The Lord wants to bring you out smelling like a rose, and for many of us there is a restoration process that He seeks to accomplish in our lives. He will redeem all your pain. And you, too, can have beauty for ashes. He wants to and He will restore all the enemy stole from you... relationships, dreams, finances, careers, gifts, health and much more.

As you might imagine one very important area of my life desperately needed restoration and that concerned my mother's and my relationship. And I am very grateful and happy to report that the Lord brought a huge measure of healing, love and restoration to my mother's and my relationship. Actually, it was after many years of no communication between us that the Lord had me contact my mother when I was quite physically ill. In our ensuing conversations we both asked forgiveness of one another for the hurts that transpired between us. Although there was not full recognition of the deep pain I experienced, there was a great deal of healing and understanding that did occur between my mother and myself for which I am so very thankful to the Lord. My mother even acknowledged that she believed the Lord told her that she never once hugged me or told me she loved me as a mother.

I love my mother very much! Indeed, she is my only mother. And very importantly, when I forgave my mother my physical health became completely restored! There is such tremendous power in exercising forgiveness toward those who hurt us and we are the beneficiaries as the Lord instructs us to do. Jeremiah 30:17 states "I will restore you to health and heal you of your wounds" and He did!

In the years after this healing I talked with my Mom about the Lord and accepting Him as Savior and having eternal life in Heaven. She stated she completely agreed with that and so I have both the hope and the faith that my dear Mom will be in Heaven with me. In fact I believe total healing and restoration of our relationship and that of all of my family will take place in Heaven. I believe the mother I did not have on earth I *will* have in Heaven! And in the meantime, the Lord continued to work His miracles in our relationship and brought a huge measure of restoration and healing to both of us. I was with able to be with my mother on a regular basis for 3 years when she suffered with severe Alzheimer's. She ended up leaving this earth and stepping into eternity in my arms. It was an honor truly to be there for her and now I have the comfort she IS with Christ in Heaven.

On another important note and for all the animal lovers out there, another aspect of my life I would like to tell you about are my pets. Animal companions can bring unconditional love, joy, peace and healing to our hearts, mind, body and souls! I am incredibly biased. I have a precious Golden Retriever and I tell you I believe they are the greatest dogs God ever made! They give such love and comfort and just love to be with their people.

So if you find yourself lonely and in need of some loving companionship, consider adopting the right breed of dog or the right pet for you. For those of us who love our dogs, they ARE part of our family for sure! They will return the love and care you give to them a thousand fold at least!

CHAPTER NINE

YOUR LIFE HAS MEANING AND PURPOSE

There is a divine purpose for your life. You have gifts and talents resident in you that the Lord wants to use for His glory. What is it that you love to do and are passionate about? Do you love to speak or write? Are you an artist or a musician? A builder? An inventor? Perhaps you are a fantastic cook and love to make special meals for people? Do you like to pray and intercede for others? What really moves you makes you smile and warms your heart?

In my case, I love to speak for the Lord. Give me a microphone and an audience of one or more and I need no preparation. I am ready to tell you how the Lord changed my life and how He can change your life for the better, too.

The Lord has a vision and a plan for your life. "For I know the plans I have for you, declares the Lord, plans to prosper you and not to harm you, plans to give you a future and a hope." (Jeremiah 29:11).

You don't want to die with your purpose unfulfilled. You want to be able to fully utilize all the gift and talents the Lord has given you for His glory. And He will. Trust Him to go before you and open the doors for you. He wants to do exceedingly abundantly more than all you can ask or imagine because that is what His Word tells us in Ephesians. "Now to Him who is able to do far more abundantly beyond all that we ask or think, according to the power that works within us..." (Ephesians 3:20). "For we are His workmanship, created in Christ Jesus for good works, which God prepared beforehand so that we would walk in them." (Ephesians 2:10). Everyone has something he or she is good at or at least enjoys doing. Listen to your heart and ask the Lord to develop your gifts, talents, and passions for His glory. He delights in doing this, for there is a whole world out there of hurting people who can use what you have to offer. These talents do not have to be deep and profound, yet they can be. A pastor I have heard preach talks about a woman in his church who loves to make pies. Making pies and giving them to hurting people is her gift of hospitality at work..

I enjoy when people tell me what they love to do. So often it is the complete opposite of what I like to do, and I just stand in amazement at the talent and gifting with which the Lord has blessed people. If we all liked and did the same thing this world would be a very boring place.

What is it that motivates and inspires you? Examine your heart. If you are not sure, ask the Lord. In addition, some churches offer spiritual gifting classes to help you assess your gifts.

If you are ever unsure of what to do or which direction to take you can take comfort in the fact the God's Word states in Psalm 32:8, "I will instruct you and teach you in the way which you should go: I will counsel you with My eye upon you." He wants to help you discover why He made you and put you on this earth. Ultimately it is for all of us to give our Creator glory…that is why we were made.

Rest assured you were made and born for a purpose and the Lord will reveal to you what that is and how you can best utilize your gifts for Him. In the process expect much personal reward and satisfaction as you sow into the lives of others. You will be amazed how your life can touch and help others. And you will be very blessed in the process as well!

CHAPTER 10

FOR THE APPLAUSE OF HEAVEN

Therefore, since we have so great a cloud of witnesses surrounding us, let us also lay aside every encumbrance, and the sin which so easily entangles us, and let us run with endurance the race that is set before us, fixing our eyes on Jesus, the author and perfecter of faith, who for the joy set before Him endured the cross, despising the shame, and has sat down at the right hand of the throne of God." (Hebrews 12:1, 2)

Run in such a way you win. You may not be aware of this but you have all of Heaven cheering you on to achieve the plans, purposes, and desires of our Father's heart for your life. He wants you to finish strong and be all you can be for Him. When we get to the end of our life and are taken "home" to Heaven we want to hear Him say "Well done, good and faithful servant" don't we? (Matthew 25:21, 23).

You and I can finish strong no matter what problems and obstacles we have run up against in our lives. Our God will help us overcome and help us be a blessing to other people in the process.

Nothing is over until God says it's over. Sometimes you just have to encourage yourself in the Lord and tell yourself you are living for the applause of Heaven. What happens, here is a minute fleck of time compared to where we will spend our time when we leave this earth...in eternity. We must not lose that perspective. What happens here on earth matters, but it is not our final resting place. Righteousness and justice are the foundation of God's throne and it is there that we will see everything wrong be made right and every relationship and body made whole. The world may not give you the recognition and thanks that are due you, but someday your Lord will. He will make everything right.

It is my sincere and fervent hope that both my life story and the principles laid out in this book will help encourage you to keep on keeping on, holding onto Christ, His Word and never giving up hope. You are precious to the Lord and very much loved. He wants you to be made whole, be touched by Him and used by Him for His glory.

If this book ministered to you in any way, or if I can pray for you, I would love to hear from you.

God bless you, My Dear Friend and Reader… You are Loved!

Christina M. Stimson, M.D.
www.gloryforhim.com

ABOUT THE AUTHOR

Christina M. Stimson, M.D. grew up in Elmhurst, Illinois, a suburb of Chicago. She attended the University of Illinois at Champaign-Urbana where she received her Bachelor of Science degree in Human Anatomy and Physiology. Christina received her Doctor of Medicine degree from the University of Illinois and is Board-certified in Internal Medicine. Christina has a powerful personal testimony of how the Lord brought her through many years of severe heartache and trials. It is her passion to encourage others and impart how the hope of holding onto the Word of God when darkness prevails can be life-changing and transforming.

Christina enjoys speaking for the Lord on TV, Christian conferences and retreats. Christina resides in Las Vegas with her precious Golden Retriever, Honey Bear, and has done missionary work in Alexandria, Egypt, Christchurch, NZ as well as the USA.